17.95

APR 1 6 2007

OCT 0 1 1998

The Indian Ocean

By **Leighton Taylor**

Featuring the photographs of
Norbert Wu

BLACKBIRCH PRESS, INC.

WOODBRIDGE, CONNECTICUT

Published by Blackbirch Press, Inc.
260 Amity Road
Woodbridge, CT 06525

©1999 by Blackbirch Press, Inc.
First Edition

e-mail: staff@blackbirch.com
Web site: www.blackbirch.com

All photographs ©Norbert Wu/Mo Yung Productions, except pages 3 (PhotoDisc), 6 and 7 (NASA).

Text ©Leighton Taylor

Printed in the United States

10 9 8 7 6 5 4 3 2 1

Editor's Note
The photos that appear on pages 13 (inset top), 16 (spear fishing), 17 (sharks), 19 (top), 20–21 and 31 (insets), page 23, show species that are found in the Indian Ocean, but the photos were taken in a different locale. Because no suitable images of the species could be found in an Indian Ocean environment, these very similar images were used instead.

Library of Congress Cataloging-in-Publication Data
Taylor, L.R. (Leighton R.)
The Indian Ocean / by Leighton Taylor; featuring the photographs of Norbert Wu
    p.   cm. — (Life in the sea)
   Includes bibliographical references and index.
   Summary: In text and photographs, presents information about the Indian Ocean, its location, physical environment, animal life, islands, and mysteries.
   ISBN 1-56711-242-0 (library binding : alk. paper)
   1. Indian Ocean—Juvenile literature. [1. Indian Ocean] I. Wu, Norbert, ill.
II. Title. III. Series: Taylor, L.R. (Leighton R.) Life in the sea.
GC721.T39   1999
551.46'7—dc21

98-19654
CIP
AC

IMAGINE A VAST, BLUE OCEAN

Imagine an ocean so large that it washes the shores of Africa, Australia, and Asia at the same time. It flows into the Pacific Ocean and also shares waters with the cold seas at the bottom of the earth, around Antarctica. Though its southern waters are very cold, the big middle part of this ocean is warm. Floating in its deep, salty waters are many islands that have rich coral reefs. Some of them once had lush, beautiful rainforests.

AN OCEAN OF TREASURES

But you don't have to imagine! The Indian Ocean is such a place!

This vast body of water has served as a "cultural highway" for centuries. For at least 1,000 years, Indian Ocean sailors have carried trade goods between Arabia, India, Africa, and even China.

Even before Columbus tried to find a new way to get to the Indian Ocean, sailing ships from Portugal had sailed there. They sailed south along the coast of Africa, went around the southern end, and then up into the Indian Ocean. Later, Dutch sailors from the Netherlands sailed there. The Portuguese and the Dutch established cities and even countries on the shores of the Indian Ocean.

Why did European explorers want to sail all the way to the Indian Ocean? Because the people who lived there sold wonderful things—spices, silk, gold, and silver. The sailors from Europe could bring those exotic goods back to Europe and sell them for a great profit.

Today we know this great ocean has many other riches. Some of these are worth more than money. These treasures are the thousands of species of living plants and animals that thrive in the waters and reefs of the Indian Ocean.

High above the reefs of Mahe Island in the Indian Ocean.
Inset right: **A beautiful sunset fills the sky over the Maldive Islands.**
Inset below: **The Indian Ocean's coral reefs are rich with plant and animal life.**

THE NATURE OF THE OCEAN

When astronauts look at Earth from space, they see a planet mostly covered by water. Some people call our Earth "Planet Ocean." That's because it has much more ocean than dry land.

From space, the world's ocean looks the same all over. But it can be very different from place to place. The water can be different. The location and shape of the holes filled by seawater can be special.

How is seawater different from one place to another? Here are three important ways that seawater can change, depending on:

1. how warm or cold it is
2. how much salt it holds
3. how clear or murky it is

Sea water in the Indian Ocean flows in complicated patterns called currents. Some currents are warmer and saltier than others. Some currents are on the surface. Some are deep.

Oceanographers are scientists who study the ocean. Oceanographers can tell a lot about the currents in the Indian Ocean by using satellites. Cameras and instruments on satellites record the temperature, movement, and level of the ocean currents on the surface of the sea. Oceanographers also use ships to take water temperatures and measure ocean saltiness below the surface.

All this information helps them do many things—study currents and the winds, predict weather, help fishermen find fish, help sea captains save fuel, and a lot more.

The Apollo Astronauts took this view of the Indian Ocean from space. The chain of islands near the bottom are the Maldives.

MORE THAN SEVEN SEAS—THE MANY WATERS OF THE WORLD

The location and shape of a basin filled by seawater gives each body of water special characteristics. The earth's seawater fits into holes of many different sizes and shapes. These giant holes are shaped by the land around them. The names for these different areas of seawater depend on their size and shape.

An *ocean* is the biggest area of seawater. An *ocean* is so big, it touches several continents. It can take many days to cross an ocean, even in a fast boat. The Pacific Ocean is the world's largest ocean. The Atlantic Ocean and the Indian Ocean are very large, too.

A *sea* is smaller than an ocean but still very big. A sea is more enclosed by land than an ocean and may touch only a few countries or even be in the middle of a single country. Sailing the "Seven Seas" is an old sailor's term. In reality, there are many more seas than seven. The Mediterranean Sea is a big, famous sea. It is connected to the Red Sea by the Suez Canal. The Caribbean Sea touches Florida and Mexico and has many islands.

NORTH AMERICA

North Pacific Ocean

Gulf of Mexico

South Pacific Ocean

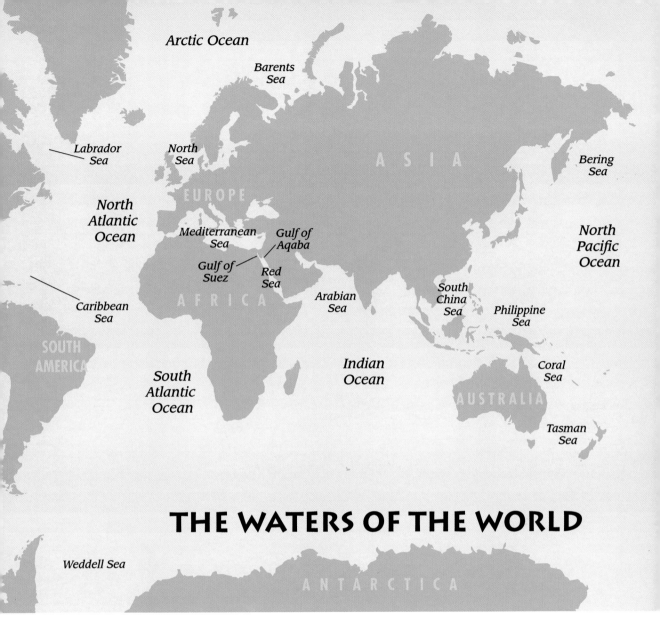

Arctic Ocean

Barents
Sea

Labrador
Sea

North
Sea

ASIA

Bering
Sea

North
Atlantic
Ocean

EUROPE

Mediterranean
Sea

Gulf of
Aqaba

North
Pacific
Ocean

Gulf of
Suez

Red
Sea

AFRICA

Arabian
Sea

South
China
Sea

Philippine
Sea

Caribbean
Sea

SOUTH
AMERICA

Indian
Ocean

Coral
Sea

South
Atlantic
Ocean

AUSTRALIA

Tasman
Sea

THE WATERS OF THE WORLD

Weddell Sea

ANTARCTICA

Smaller parts of the ocean can be called a *gulf*. Sometimes gulfs are big, sometimes small. The Gulf of Mexico is very big. The Gulf of Aqaba (AH-ka-ba) and the Gulf of Suez are small. These gulfs are at the very top of the Red Sea.

RICH REEFS AND WARM WINDS

Most of the Indian Ocean is warm. It lies in the tropics and gets plenty of sunshine. Warm winds blow across the ocean and make the water move in currents. The warm waters, bright sunshine, and shallow depths around the islands and coasts make the Indian Ocean a very good place for coral reefs.

Almost every island has coral reefs around it. These reefs contain thousands of species of corals, fishes, sponges, anemones, starfish, and sharks. They are perfect habitats for nearly every kind of tropical sea creature. There are many more kinds of reef animals in the Indian Ocean than in the Caribbean Sea.

For a snorkeler or scuba diver, it's really hard to choose the best place to dive in the Indian Ocean. There are so many dramatic underwater spaces and rich reefs swarming with life. The Seychelles and Maldive Islands are very popular spots. Many diving tourists travel long distances—from Europe, America, Australia, and Africa—to swim with the marine life in these island reefs.

The brightly colored coral reefs of the Indian Ocean are teeming with nearly every kind of marine life.

LIVING ON THE EDGE

True or False?

All fish and crabs live only in the water.

No trees ever live in the ocean.

Well, the answer for both statements is "partly true and partly false." That's because some plants and animals live on the edge, between land and sea. They spend part of their time in both places.

Ghost crabs live on sandy beaches. They dig holes in the sand and stay in them until the tide comes up. They scurry sideways back and forth along the beach looking for food. As the waves crash up on the shore, food is washed in for the crabs.

Coconut palms grow very near the same sandy beaches where ghost crabs live. Their broad leaves and coconuts hang over the waves. Coconuts are the seeds of a coconut tree. Sometimes coconuts drop into the seawater and float off to grow on other islands.

Indian Ocean coastlines have sandy beaches. But they also have special low forests that grow in the water at the edge of the land. The trees in these forests are called mangroves. They grow in places where rivers meet the ocean, where the water is not quite as salty as seawater. A mix of freshwater and seawater is called *brackish* water. Many animals live around the wet roots of mangrove trees.

When the tide takes the water out, the muddy bottom around the mangroves meets the air. Fiddler crabs rush around on the mud, waving their big claws. Each is engaged in a fight with other crabs for a place to live. Mudskipper gobies hop around on the mud. They even climb the mangrove trees! These small fish with big buggy eyes look easy to catch. But they aren't. They move fast on the mud and in the roots and branches of mangroves.

Opposite: **A ghost crab scurries along a sandy shore.**
Inset top: **Mudskippers inhabit the muddy areas of mangroves.**
Inset bottom: **Some coconut palms live so near the ocean that they drop their seeds (coconuts) in the water.**

IN AND OUT OF SCHOOL

Why do fish swim in schools? Is it to learn new things? Maybe, but scientists think there are other reasons that fish swim in large groups.

One of the main reasons for schooling has to do with survival. Every fish in a school gets protection. Some hunting animals see the school as one big, scary shape—instead of a group of many small, individual fish. Other hunters get confused and can't pick out a fish to eat. Their attention shifts from one fast fish to another to another to another. By the time a predator has made up its mind, often the school has gotten away.

If a schooling fish somehow looks different—if it is sick and slow, or has a wound or spot—a predator can often focus on that fish and snatch it.

Some plant-eating surgeonfish schools form a bullying gang. A feisty damselfish can scare off one or two surgeonfish from the patch of plants it lives near. But when a school of 15-20 surgeonfish rush in, the damselfish gives up and the surgeonfish eat the deserted plants.

A diver swims with a school of bigeyes.
Inset: **A huge school of fusiliers and blue-lined snappers swarms along a coral wall.**

← **Humans are many fishes' most dangerous predators.**

HUNTERS WITH FINS.
HUNTERS WITH LEGS.

Ocean predators take on many shapes. In the Indian Ocean, fish are vulnerable to attack from all sorts of enemies—some of which don't live or swim in the ocean at all.

Humans, who hunt all sorts of fish in the Indian Ocean, are a common predator. Some prey with spears, others set traps and wait for their prey to come to them.

Of course, the ocean is filled with many more conventional predators, as well. Sharks, in particular, are some of the ocean's most efficient and skilled hunters. Other highly effective killers include poisonous animals, such as lionfish, stonefish, and banded sea snakes.

Top left: **Seychelles fishers set their traps before throwing them overboard.**
Top right: **Lionfish in the Indian Ocean show off their fancy, but poisonous spines to keep away their predators.**
Right: **A grey reef shark joins a school of jacks as they feed in the ocean current.**

◀ This school of blue-green chromis finds shelter in a patch of staghorn coral.

BETWEEN CORAL AND A HARD PLACE

India is one of the most densely populated countries in the world. In its largest cities, there are not enough houses or apartments for the millions who live there.

There is something of a housing shortage on the Indian Ocean's coral reefs, as well. There are so many kinds of animals living there that finding a place to live—and guarding it—is hard and constant work. Some animals live in the sand. But most reef animals find places to hide and rest inside the reef itself. Some find shelter on other animals or in between the branches of sea plants.

Corals, sponges, sea fans, and their relatives provide homes for many other animals. As they grow upward and outward, hard corals form caves and cracks. Different kinds of animals seek shelter inside these spaces. There, they hide from predators and find safe places to breed. Other animals—moray eels and groupers, for example—hunt in the reef's cracks and caves. Although it's dark in the cracks, eels can find hidden animals by smelling them. Eels, groupers, and other hunting fish also hide in the cracks of the reef waiting to ambush prey.

Many fish swim and feed during the day and hide in the reef at night. Parrotfish cover themselves with a kind of mucus sleeping bag when they retire for the evening. The bag seals in their smell so hunting eels can't find them.

Above: **Parrotfish cover themselves with a mucus bag at night to prevent predators from smelling them.** *Below:* **These cardinalfish get protection from the sharp spines of the sea urchins around them.**

LIVING FOSSILS?

Imagine seeing a live dinosaur walking through the woods! Such a sight would be very exciting, but very improbable. We only know about real dinosaurs from their fossil bones left in rocks. The last dinosaurs died almost 65 million years ago.

From other fossils, scientists know about ancient fishes and sharks that lived before the dinosaurs. In the Indian Ocean, about 60 years ago, a fisherman and a woman scientist caught a special fish near the Comoros Islands. The fish was big— about 3 feet (1 meter) long. It had big eyes and rough scales. Its fins looked a lot like legs instead of fish fins.

No one had ever seen this fish alive before. But they had seen ancient fossils of it that were older than dinosaur fossils. Catching such a fish was like catching a dinosaur! It was a very exciting discovery. Since then, scientists have caught more of these fish. But they have only been caught in one place in the Indian Ocean—nowhere else in the world. We are learning a lot about the history of fish, sharks, and land animals from these "living fossils."

This special fish is called a coelacanth (SEEL-A-CANTH). That name means "hollow spines." The fossil coelacanths—relatives of the living ones from the Indian Ocean— have hollow spines in their fins.

Coelacanths have only been caught in one place in the Indian Ocean.

SUCKERS ON LAND AND SEA

On Indian Ocean reefs and mud flats live many kinds of fish called gobies. Every kind of goby has a fin on its chest or stomach in the shape of a suction cup.

Gobies that live on rocks where the waves crash use their suction cup to hang on to rocks. Gobies that live on the sand use their suction cup fin to boost themselves up

Wire coral gobies live only on the branches of wire coral.

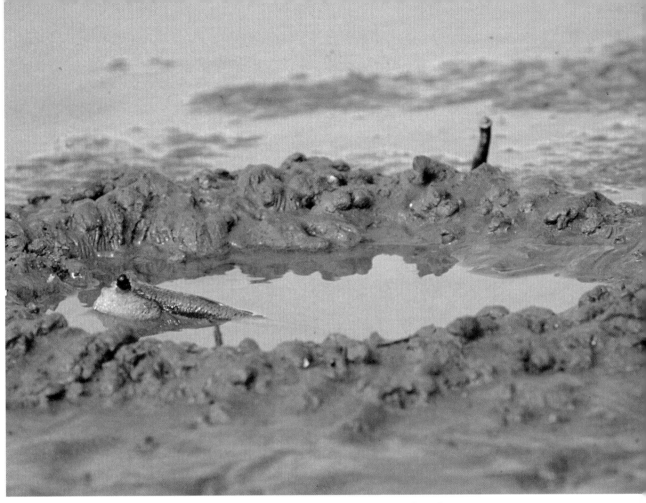

◀ **Mudskipper gobies are fish that walk on land.**

so they can use their big round eyes to see more of what's around them. Wire coral gobies live only on the branches of wire corals on coral reefs. They use their sucking fin to hang on when currents are strong.

Mudskippers are gobies that walk on land. At low tide, mudskipper gobies use their suction fin and arm-like pectoral fins to climb up tree trunks. They hop around on muddy and sandy bottoms when the tide has gone out. Mudskippers look a lot like long skinny frogs in the mud. But they aren't frogs, they are fish.

E SHARK DOUBLE-TAKES

Everybody knows what a shark looks like. It's gray with big, sharp teeth and a pointed dorsal fin, right? Not always. A lot of sharks fit the classic description, but many other sharks are quite different. Sharks can be small and colorfully patterned. They often stay still and calm on the bottom. Some have small rounded teeth. Many of these kinds of sharks live on the reefs of the Indian Ocean.

Some sharks have the ability to camouflage themselves. Their color matches their surroundings as they lie quietly on the sand or near the reef. This camouflage protects them from bigger, hunting fish. It also hides them so they can ambush and catch animals that they want to eat.

Top: **This nurse shark looks like a "typical" shark.**
Right: **This catshark is marked like a leopard.**
Opposite top: **The zebra horn shark's markings resemble the land animal that shares its name.**
Opposite bottom: **Wobbegongs are flat, feathery-looking fish that are actually a species of shark.**

Sharks that live on the ocean bottom and in caves have strong muscles around their mouths and gills. These muscles pump dissolved air across their gills so that they can breathe without swimming.  Some large swimming sharks must stay in almost constant motion—they need to swim to get enough dissolved air to breathe.

Many sharks that live on the ocean bottom lay eggs. Baby sharks are called pups. One pup hatches out of each egg. All sharks—no matter where they live—have good teeth so that they can grab their food. Some sharks eat fish and squid. Others eat clams, shrimp, and worms.

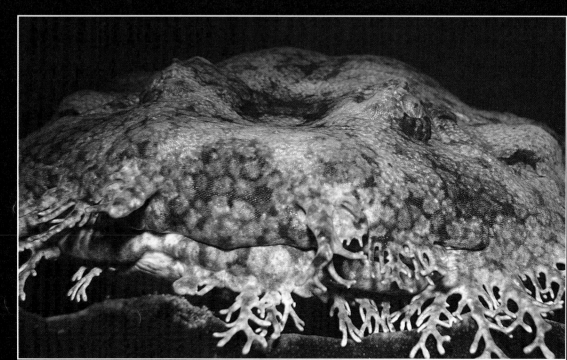

WHEN A WHALE
IS A SHARK

What is the largest fish in the world? Where does it live? Is it dangerous?

To answer these questions, remember that scientists consider sharks to be a kind of fish. All fish, including sharks and rays, have jaws, fins, and breathe by using gills.

There are many kinds of fairly large fish in the world's oceans. Swordfish can be longer than 12 feet (3.6 meters). Manta rays can weigh almost a ton. Tiger sharks can grow to 18 feet (5.5 meters) long. A big tuna weighs as much as half a car.

But the largest fish in the world is the whale shark. Whale sharks live in warm seas of the world, including the Indian Ocean. One of the best places to see whale sharks is near Australia in the Indian Ocean. There, people have seen whale sharks that are longer than a school bus!

Whale sharks get their name for two reasons—they grow to the size of big whales, and they feed mostly on krill (small shrimpy animals) and tiny fish the way some whales do. Despite the "whale" in their name, they are still sharks.

Whale sharks are the largest fish in the ocean. Some grow to be longer than a school bus.

◄ **Porcelain crabs make sticky nets out of mucus that they use to trap food.**

NETTERS AND SMASHERS

Almost all crabs and their relatives have strong claws. But different kinds of crabs use their claws in very different ways. Some crabs use the pinchers on their claws to grab worms and tiny animals to eat. Other crabs—such as fiddlers—use claws mainly to send "messages" to other crabs. They use their claws like warning flags.

One kind of crab on the Indian Ocean reefs uses its claws in a very creative way to get food. The porcelain crab makes a big, sticky web of mucus with its mouth. Then it stretches the sticky net between its claws and holds the net out into the water. When tiny food and plant animals float by, they get stuck in the mucus net. Then the crab stuffs the food-filled net into its mouth.

Mantis shrimp are relatives of shrimp. They have long, strong claws with strong muscles. A mantis shrimp uses its claws in a much less delicate way than its crab relatives. With a very hard blow, it smashes the shells of snails and crabs. This powerful shock stuns the prey and cracks it shell. Then the mantis shrimp can pick up the broken snail or crab and eat it. A mantis shrimp can hit hard enough to break the glass in an aquarium!

Mantis shrimp use their powerful front claws to smash open the shells of their prey.

A STARFISH THAT EATS CORAL

The tiny animals that build the stony structures we know as "coral" are called polyps. Certain reef animals like to feed on polyps when they want food. Butterflyfish with strong bristly teeth can pluck the individual coral polyps. Parrotfish can scrape the stony skeleton away to get at the fleshy polyps. These fish don't do very much damage to a coral colony. They only eat a few polyps at a time.

But there is no escape from the Crown of Thorns starfish. This animal got its name from the poisonous thorny spines all over its body. They reminded a biologist of the crown of thorns the Romans put on Christ when he was crucified.

A Crown of Thorns starfish eats corals by pushing its stomach out through its mouth. The stomach covers the coral skeleton and digests the coral animals directly. When it is finished eating, the Crown of Thorns starfish pulls its stomach back into its body through its mouth. When there are many of them, these starfish can destroy a big part of a coral reef.

A Crown of Thorns starfish feeds on a coral bed.
Inset left: **A close-up of the starfish's "thorns."**
Inset right: **A diver inspects a triton snail that has attacked a Crown of Thorns starfish.**

A special kind of sea snail is one animal that preys on Crown of Thorns starfish. This big snail, called a triton snail, kills and eats these starfish, despite their spines. Unfortunately, triton shells are very popular with shell collectors. On some reefs, too many tritons have been captured. In those places, the Crown of Thorns starfish escape being eaten and they overpopulate the reef. Then they overeat the coral reefs, causing the coral colonies to die. This is only one example of how human actions can seriously disturb the balance of life in nature.

GENERALISTS AND SPECIALISTS

Some reef animals are very picky about where they live. Garden eels will only live in sand with grains of a certain size. Wire gobies will only live on special kinds of wire coral.

But the candy cane starfish lives in a wide variety of places. It lives and feeds on sea fans, on corals, and even on sandy bottoms.

Scientists call animals that live in special places and eat special things "specialists." They call animals with a wide variety of foods and living places "generalists." When times get tough—with storms, pollution, or very cold temperatures—generalists stand a better chance of surviving than do specialists.

The candy cane sea star is one of the Indian Ocean's most adaptable survivors. These photos show it surrounded by a variety of coral environments.

LIGHTS, CAMERA, COLOR!

Most of the pictures of coral reefs that we see are filled with bright colors—yellow fish, red fish, blue fish, yellow sponges, purple sea fans, blue sponges. But when a scuba diver swims deep down a reef cliff and looks, the colors are gone! The reef looks dull blue and gray. The red fish look greenish. The sea fans are black or gray. Where did all the color go?

To answer, we need to know that seawater changes light. Seawater scatters light and slows it down. When sunlight shines into seawater it gets changed. The deeper sunlight goes into the water, the more it changes. Light that makes red color disappears at about 20 feet (6 meters) deep. Yellow is gone by 30 feet (9 meters).

Bright flashes are needed to capture the true colors of a deep-water reef.

Finally, only blue is left. By 2,000 feet (610 meters) deep in the Indian Ocean all light is gone and the sea is pitch black.

Because seawater changes sunlight, underwater photographers must take their own lights with them when they dive deep on Indian Ocean reefs. Powerful strobe lights flash bright light when the camera's shutter is clicked. The bright light has all the colors of sunlight so the camera sees all the colors in the reef.

◀ **Without the powerful light of a strobe, the brilliant colors of angelfish (top left), blue tangs (top right) and basslets in a coral bed would be lost in photographs.**

◀ **The wobbegong doesn't look like a shark, but it is one. Its flat and feathery appearance blends perfectly with the sandy, rocky ocean floor.**

THE UNSEEN SCENE

Camouflage is the art of not being seen. In nature, many plants and animals use this skill in order to survive. These organisms have found that the best way to stay alive is to stay hidden.

Different animals use their camouflage abilities in different ways. Some—such as the venomous stonefish, the sharp-toothed crocodilefish, or the wobbegong shark—use their natural disguises to become invisible to their prey. Blending in with their surroundings, these hunters lie in wait for an unsuspecting fish or other creature to swim by.

Other camouflage artists use their disguises to prevent their being eaten. When they remain motionless, pipefish look just like seaweed. Small decorator crabs cover themselves with sponges that make them nearly invisible on a colorful coral reef.

The deadly stonefish sits motionless below a coral-covered boulder, waiting for prey to happen by. *Inset:* This scorpionfish is colorfully mottled and resembles a coral-covered rock.

ISLANDS OF OLD

The islands in the Indian Ocean vary greatly in size and age. Some islands are big. The island of Madagascar (MAD-A-GAS-CAR), off the southeast coast of India, is the fourth-largest island in the world. Some islands are small. You could walk across some of the low flat islands in the Maldive group in ten minutes.

Some Indian Ocean islands are young. Volcanoes made them only a few million years ago. That's young for a piece of land on Earth! The Seychelles Islands and Sri Lanka (this big island used to be called Ceylon), however, are pieces of an ancient continent (called Gondwanaland) that broke apart hundreds of millions of years ago. Before this ancient continent broke up, there was no Indian Ocean.

An aerial view of a coral atoll in the Seychelles.
Inset: **Coral sand and volcanic rocks line the shores of many Indian Ocean islands.**

◄ **The lush foliage of the islands provides homes for many species of tree frogs.**

ISLANDS OF LOST WORLDS

The waters of the Indian Ocean hold many strange and wonderful creatures. So, too, do the islands that sit in those waters. The Seychelles Island is the only place in the world where the Coco de Mer grows. This strange black coconut looks like the pelvis of a woman. In the forests around these odd coco palm trees live neon-colored tree frogs and long, thin bugs that look like sticks.

Giant tortoises bigger than coffee tables march slowly around the low, flat island of Aldabra—they share the island with thousands of birds.

Scientists are not certain how these tortoises got to Aldabra—they don't like to swim in the ocean.

Some worlds are truly lost. Many giant, thick-headed birds called dodos once lived on the island of Mauritius. These birds were taller than adult humans, but are now extinct. The last one was killed 200 years ago.

Left: **Coco de Mer is only found on Praslin Island in the Seychelles.** *Below:* **This insect, called a walking stick, is one of the Seychelles's most successful land camouflagers.**

SAILS OF THE INDIES

Boats and sailors have used the wind to travel the Indian Ocean for at least 2,000 years. For almost all that time, they have used a kind of wooden sailboat called a dhow (DOW). Dhows have a unique triangular sail and slanted mast called a lateen rig.

The Indian Ocean is a good place to sail these boats. For half of the year, the winds blow from India to Africa. For the other half, they blow from Africa to India. These two-way winds are called monsoon winds. They are an important feature of the Indian Ocean and the countries around it.

Dhows have carried trade goods between Africa, India, China, and the Indian Ocean islands for centuries. Dhows still sail the same waters. Today's dhows are built the same way as they were many, many years ago. Strong mangrove ribs form the boat's shape. The ribs are planked with African mahogany wood. Cracks between the planks are stuffed with coconut fiber soaked in oil from shark livers. This stuffing helps to stop leaks.

Centuries ago, dhows carried things of great value to people around the Indian Ocean—African hippo teeth, rhino horns, exotic fruits, Chinese dishes and figurines, Arabian furniture, dates, and carpets.

Today's dhows carry cheaper, basic goods—canned food, shoes, tea, sugar, clothing, and lumber. Big ships and airplanes carry most of the expensive products across the Indian Ocean now. But dhows are still an important way for island people to get the goods they need.

Opposite: **Dhows use special triangular sails and slanted masts to capture the strong trade winds on the Indian Ocean.**
Right: **Simple boats transport the people who fish the waters for a living.**

GOING UP?

Many people are worried that the level of the world's oceans is rising. Scientists have measured slight increases—much less than an inch a year—during the last 25 years.

But how can the ocean level be rising? Where is the water coming from? Warmer weather may be melting the ice caps near the North and South poles. As melting ice drips more and more water into the ocean, the level rises slowly.

But why is it getting warmer? There may be several reasons. Perhaps the warming of the earth (called "global warming" in the news) is part of a natural cycle. Humans may be causing the earth to warm up, too. We burn lots and lots of forests in South America and in Southeast Asia. We burn lots and lots of gasoline and oil to run cars and power plants. But it is not heat from the burning that warms the earth. It is the smoke—or at least some of the gases in the smoke. The worst gas is carbon dioxide. This and other gases are part of normal air. But all of our burning is making more and more carbon dioxide, which makes the earth hold more heat. The increased heat may be warming up the earth and melting the polar ice.

The 263,000 people who live on the Maldive Islands in the Indian Ocean are especially worried about rising sea levels. Most of these 1,180 islands are less than 3 feet (1 meter) above sea level. If sea level rises 3 feet in the next 100 years—as some scientists think it might—most of the Maldives will be gone, or at least flooded out.

APPENDIX A:
HOW DO YOU MAP AN OCEAN?

A taxi driver can find an address by using a map and street signs. But how can a sailor find a location on the broad, empty ocean? When a boat sails near land, sailors can recognize landmarks. A map, or even a drawing of mountains and cliffs and beaches, can help them find their way. Some of the first maps made by sailors were made on the Red Sea. We know that the Egyptian Queen Hatshepsut sailed the length of the Red Sea about 2,500 years ago.

But in the open sea, away from land, there aren't any signs. And how can you make a map of a place that is all ocean?

Here's how: All mapmakers have agreed on two kinds of imaginary lines that cover the earth. One set of lines go from the top of the earth—at the North Pole—to the bottom of the earth—at the South Pole. These are the lines of "longitude" (lonj-EH-tood). The other lines go around the earth from east to west. These are the lines of "latitude" (lat-EH-tood). The latitude line that goes around the fattest part of the earth (at its middle) is the called the equator. Above the equator is the Northern half of the earth, also known as the Northern Hemisphere. Below the equator is the Southern part of the earth. That's the Southern Hemisphere.

The equator is easy to find on a globe. But mapmakers also divide the earth in half going north to south. This line divides the world into two halves, too—the western half and the eastern half. Every line is numbered with degrees as they move around the circular earth.

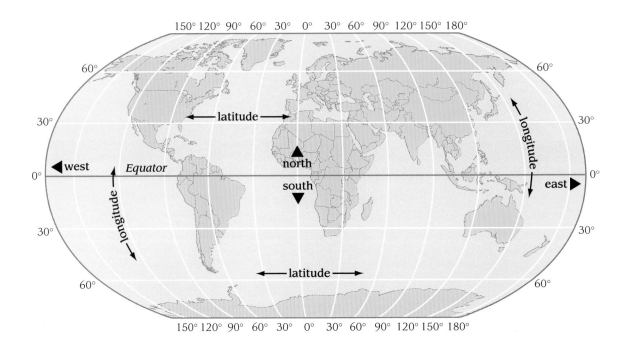

You can find the Indian Ocean on a map of the world by using "positions." A position is the place where a particular place on the latitude and a particular place on the longitude meet.

Find the longitude line for 80 degrees east. Find the latitude line for 8 degrees north. The two lines will cross just south of India in the Indian Ocean.

But such lines only appear on maps. Nobody can actually draw them on the ocean! So how do sailors find their positions? By looking at the sky! At any given time, the moon, stars, and the sun are in predictable places. If a navigator knows what time it is and can measure the location of the sun, moon, or a few stars, he or she can find a position on Earth.

A new and even easier way has recently been invented. Navigators can use small computers that use satellites instead of stars to find a position of latitude and longitude.

GLOSSARY

adaptation A special way to survive that an animal inherits from its ancestors.

ambush To hide and then suddenly attack.

brackish Water that is too salty to drink but not as salty as seawater.

current A small or large body of water that is moving slower or faster than the water around it.

dhow A special kind of Arab sail-boat.

Equator The imaginary line of latitude that goes around the waist of the Earth (from east to west).

gulf A large part of an ocean or sea that reaches into the land.

latitude Imaginary line that goes around the earth from east to west (side to side). Map makers draw them on maps to show where places are located.

longitude Imaginary lines that go around the earth from north to south (up to down). Map makers draw them on maps to show where places are located.

navigation A mathematical way to find exactly where you are (your **position**) by using latitude and longitude.

oceanographer A scientist who studies the ocean and seas— including their currents, waves, plants and animals.

polyp One tiny coral animal. Many coral polyps make up a coral colony, or group.

position The exact place where someone or something is, described as a point where a specific latitude and specific longitude meet.

salinity The amount of chemicals dissolved in seawater. The salinity of pure water is zero; the salinity of seawater is more than 3%.

FURTHER READING

Bramwell, Martyn. *The Oceans* (Earth Science Library). Danbury, CT: Franklin Watts, Inc., 1994.

Clarke, Penny. *Beneath the Oceans* (Worldwise series). Danbury, CT: Franklin Watts, Inc., 1997.

Penny, Malcolm. *The Indian Ocean* (Seas and Oceans series). Chatham, NJ: Raintree/Steck-Vaughn, 1997.

Ricciuti, Edward R. *Fish* (Our Living World series). Woodbridge, CT: Blackbirch Press, 1993.

Savage, Stephen. *Animals of the Oceans* (Animals by Habitat series). Chatham, NJ: Raintree/Steck-Vaughn, 1997.

INDEX